STRAWBERRIES

ELAINE ELLIOT

Photography by Julian Beveridge

FORMAC PUBLISHING COMPANY LIMITED
HALIFAX 1998

PHOTO CREDITS:
All photographs by Julian Beveridge except where noted below:
Nova Scotia Dept. of Agriculture and Marketing: p. 4; p. 5.

PARTICIPATING RESTAURANTS:
A. Hiram Walker Estate Heritage Inn,
  St. Andrews, NB
Acton's Grill and Café, Wolfville, NS
Algonquin Hotel, St. Andrews, NB
Amherst Shore Country Inn, Lorneville, NS
Bluenose Lodge, Lunenburg, NS
Carriage House Inn, Fredericton, NB
Catherine McKinnon's Spot O' Tea, Stanley
  Bridge, PEI
Darlington's on Duke, Halifax, NS
Dundee Arms, Charlottetown, PEI
Falcourt Inn, Nictaux, NS
Harbourview Inn, Smiths Cove, NS
Hotel Beauséjour, Moncton, NB
Hotel Halifax, Halifax, NS
Inn on the Lake, Waverley, NS
Kaulback House Historic Inn,
  Lunenburg, NS
Liscombe Lodge, Liscomb Mills, NS
Loon Bay Lodge, St. Stephen, NB
Mountain Gap Inn and Resort,
  Smiths Cove, NS
Murray Manor Bed and Breakfast,
  Yarmouth, NS
Palliser Restaurant, Truro, NS
Pansy Patch, St. Andrews, NB
Planters' Barracks Country Inn,
  Starrs Point, NS
Prince Edward Hotel,
  Charlottetown, PEI
Salmon River House Country Inn,
  Salmon River, NS
Seasons in Thyme, Summerside, PEI
Steamers Stop Inn, Gagetown, NB
West Point Lighthouse, West Point, PEI
Wickwire House Bed and Breakfast, Kentville, NS

Dedication:
This book is dedicated to my husband Robert and our sons, thanking them for their continued encouragement and support.

Copyright © 1998 by Formac Publishing Company Limited

Formac Publishing Company acknowledges the support of the Department of Canadian Heritage and the Nova Scotia Department of Education and Culture in the development of writing and publishing in Canada.

Canadian Cataloguing in Publication Data
Elliot, Elaine, 1939-
    Strawberries
    (Maritime flavours)
    Includes index.
    ISBN 0-88780-418-7
1. Cookery (Strawberries). 2. Cookery, Canadian — Maritime Provinces.
I. Beveridge, Julian. II. Title. III. Series.
TX813.S9E44 1998   641.6'475   C97-950250-7

Formac Publishing Company Limited
5502 Atlantic Street
Halifax, N.S.
B3H 1G4

Printed in China

CONTENTS

INTRODUCTION

*F*ollowing the theme of the internationally successful Maritime Flavours series, I feel it is fitting that the noble strawberry be featured in this book, the seventh one in the set. To provide these delicious recipes I contacted the chefs of the many inns and restaurants of the region and again they have generously shared with us the pleasures of their tables. I thank them. In order to write a well-rounded cookbook, I have added a few tried and true recipes from my personal collection. The recipes have been tested and adjusted to serve four to six adults.

Fine food presentation is an art, one which is receiving increased emphasis from our chefs. Many of the dishes featured in this book were photographed on site — what better way to show how these recipes are presented by their originators!

Mmmm, the wonderful, sweet strawberry.

Have you ever met anyone who didn't love strawberries? In the Maritimes, strawberries herald the arrival of summer around the end of June, with the harvest lasting three to four weeks. While fresh berries are delivered to farm markets and grocery stores daily during berry season, I can think of no finer way to while away a morning than to head off to a berry patch. U-pick berry operations are very popular, giving us an opportunity to pick the freshest berries of the crop.

Imported varieties from California, Florida, and Mexico are available in supermarkets throughout the year, and while they might lack the special flavour of local berries just picked, they can brighten a winter menu. Sweetened and unsweetened berries are always available in the freezer section of supermarkets. While the freezing process causes the berries to soften slightly, they are excellent for use in recipes requiring cooked or puréed fruit.

VARIETIES

The many varieties of strawberries have distinct characteristics. In the Maritimes, the early Veestar produces medium sized berries with an excellent flavour, while the Annapolis variety produces larger berries with a less intense flavour. Of the midseason crop, the popular Glooscap produces medium to large red fruit with a good flavour, while the Kent variety produces a high yield of large, red fruit. And for those who are afraid they have missed berry season, look for Bounty, or Cavendish, a late berry medium to large in size, sweet, and full of flavour.

CARE

Like most small fruit, strawberries are perishable, and for optimum flavour should be consumed shortly after harvest. Strawberries do not ripen after being picked, so you should look for firm, plump red berries with bright green caps. Arrange unwashed strawberries on paper towel in a shallow pan. Cover loosely and refrigerate, unwashed, for up to two days. At serving time, gently rinse, pat dry and then remove caps or hulls.

While frozen berries lose some of their colour and texture, the flavour is a wonderful reminder of summer. Cool berries before freezing, as this will decrease their water loss

when thawed. Rinse berries in cool water, drain well, and hull. For each 4 cups of berries, add 3/4 cup sugar and toss lightly. Package in desired amounts, leaving 1 inch of headspace in containers; seal and freeze immediately. If you prefer to freeze your berries without sugar, place whole cleaned and hulled berries in a single layer on a tray in the freezer. When frozen, package in freezer bags and return to the freezer. While they may lose some of their vitamin C content, these strawberries should keep their shape and colour for up to a year, and can replace fresh berries in most recipes.

NUTRITIONAL VALUE

Fresh strawberries are an excellent source of vitamin C, contain potassium, and are a source of dietary fibre. They are low in sodium, have no cholesterol, and a one–cup serving contains only 76 calories.

Sixteenth-century author William Butler captured our thoughts when he said, "Doubtless God could have made a better berry, but doubtless God never did." Whether you start your day with French toast stuffed with strawberries or end it with a delectable strawberry dessert, there is something for everyone in this book. Enjoy!

BREAKFAST OR BRUNCH

*W*hat better way to start your day than with a bowl of fresh strawberries? Perhaps you would like to spread Grace Swan's Best Ever Strawberry Jam on your morning muffin, or maybe you would prefer to sample Wickwire House Stuffed French Toast.

◄ *Wickwire House French Toast is stuffed with cheese, bananas, and strawberries*

WICKWIRE HOUSE STUFFED FRENCH TOAST

WICKWIRE HOUSE BED AND BREAKFAST, KENTVILLE, NS

Innkeepers Darlene and Jim Peerless of Wickwire House serve their French toast as a pocket filled with cheese, bananas, and succulent strawberries.

1 loaf Italian style bread

1/3 cup spreadable strawberry flavoured cream cheese

1/3 cup strawberries, diced

1/4 cup banana, diced

4 extra-large eggs

4 tablespoons light cream or milk

2 tablespoons powdered or confectioners' sugar

Strawberry Sauce, recipe follows

Cut bread into 4 slices, each 1 1/2 inches thick. Make a pocket in each slice by cutting crosswise from the bottom almost to the top. In a small bowl combine cream cheese, strawberries, and bananas and divide between each bread pocket. In a wide shallow pan beat eggs with cream or milk. Add stuffed bread slices, one at a time, and allow to stand long enough to absorb some of the egg mixture, then turn over to coat the other side.

Lightly grease a large non-stick skillet and heat to 325–350°F. Add bread slices and cook until brown; turn and brown other side. Remove from pan and dust with powdered sugar. To serve, top each serving with Strawberry Sauce. Serves 4.

Strawberry Sauce

2 cups fresh or frozen strawberries

2–3 tablespoons sugar

Combine strawberries and sugar in a blender or food processor and purée. Yields 1 1/2 cups sauce.

STRAWBERRY PECAN MUFFINS

Serve these muffins warm from the oven. It is doubtful that any will be left over, but they reheat beautifully in a microwave.

3/4 cup all-purpose flour

3/4 cup whole wheat flour

2 teaspoons baking powder

1/2 teaspoon cinnamon

1/2 teaspoon salt

1/2 cup finely chopped pecans

1 egg

1/2 cup brown sugar

1 cup milk

1/4 cup vegetable oil

1 teaspoon vanilla

1 cup fresh strawberries, chopped

Preheat oven to 375°F. Coat a muffin pan with non-stick spray or line with paper liners.

Combine flours, baking powder, cinnamon, salt, and pecans in a large bowl, and mix well. In a separate bowl, whisk together the egg, brown sugar, milk, oil, and vanilla. Add the flour mixture and stir gently until well blended; fold in strawberries. Fill muffin pans 3/4 full. Bake 20–25 minutes, or until lightly golden brown and a toothpick inserted in the centre comes out clean. Yields 12 muffins.

BEST EVER STRAWBERRY JAM

BLUENOSE LODGE, LUNENBURG, NS

Innkeeper Grace Swan says that this homemade strawberry jam is one of the most popular items on the Inn's breakfast buffet. Guests frequently request her recipe, which requires less sugar than many other jams.

2 1/2 pounds strawberries (2 very full quart boxes)

2 cups sugar

1 package Garden Fare freezer jam gelling powder

Mash berries in a large bowl. Incorporate sugar into berry mixture, stirring to dissolve completely. Allow berries to stand at room temperature for 20 minutes, stirring occasionally. Sprinkle gelling powder over berries, a little at a time, stirring until it is completely dissolved. Let stand overnight, then bottle in sterilized jars. Refrigerate for immediate use or store in freezer for up to one year. Yields 6 cups jam.

FRESH STRAWBERRY BUTTER

What better way to start the day than with a freshly baked muffin or bagel topped with delicious Strawberry Butter? I suggest you store any unused butter in the freezer, where it will keep beautifully for several months.

1/2 cup fresh strawberries, rinsed, hulled, and patted dry

1 cup unsalted butter

2 tablespoons icing sugar

Blend together all ingredients in a small bowl or food processor until the mixture is pale pink. Use immediately or store in the freezer in an airtight container. Yields 1 1/4 cups.

Best Ever Strawberry Jam is a popular treat at the Bluenose Lodge in Lunenburg, NS ▶

ENTRÉES AND ACCOMPANIMENTS

*W*ho says that strawberries

are only for dessert? Our innovative chefs have a variety

of first course options for the daring home gourmet!

◄ *Chef Helmut Pflueger's Poached Salmon with Strawberry Leek Sauce*

POACHED SALMON WITH STRAWBERRY LEEK SAUCE

INN ON THE LAKE, WAVERLEY, NS

Ever conscious of using fresh fruits and vegetables in season, chef Helmut Pflueger developed this delicious poached salmon dish, complemented by a Strawberry Leek Sauce.

6 black peppercorns

1/2 teaspoon salt

1/2 lemon, sliced

2 cups water

4 boneless salmon filets, 6 ounces each

Strawberry Leek Sauce

4 teaspoons sugar

1 1/2 cup white wine

2 teaspoons balsamic vinegar

6–8 pink peppercorns

8 large strawberries, hulled and sliced

1 leek, white part only, thinly sliced

salt and pepper, to taste

4 tablespoons cold butter

Prepare poaching liquid by combining peppercorns, salt, lemon slices, and water and bringing to a simmer. Gently poach salmon, allowing approximately 10 minutes per inch of salmon thickness.

While salmon is poaching, prepare Strawberry Leek Sauce. Place sugar, wine, vinegar, pink peppercorns, strawberry and leek slices in a sauté pan and bring to a boil. Reduce heat and cook for 2 minutes. Season with salt and pepper, then whisk in cold butter, stirring until sauce begins to thicken. To serve, place salmon filets on plates and nap with sauce. Serves 4.

ELEGANT CHOCOLATE-DIPPED STRAWBERRIES

A. HIRAM WALKER ESTATE HERITAGE INN, ST. ANDREWS, NB

Elizabeth Cooney serves these delectable large strawberries for her afternoon high tea. If the strawberries are extra large, you might find them double dipped, one half in brown chocolate and the other half in white chocolate.

15–20 large strawberries

1/2 cup semi-sweet dark or white chocolate

6 tablespoons pure maple syrup

Choose only the most perfect large strawberries and rinse and pat dry, leaving the green hulls intact.

In a small bowl combine chocolate and maple syrup. Microwave on medium, stirring at 30–second intervals until chocolate melts and maple syrup is incorporated, approximately 90 seconds. Gently dip strawberries in chocolate and place to harden on waxed paper.
Serves 4–6.

STRAWBERRY AND APPLE COMPOTE

PRINCE EDWARD HOTEL, CHARLOTTETOWN, PEI

Chef Joerg Solterman finds that this delicious condiment complements many chicken or pork dishes, especially those prepared for summer barbecues.

1 Granny Smith apple, cored and diced

2 red delicious apples, cored and diced

3/4 cup lemon juice

1 1/2 cups sugar

1/4 cup balsamic vinegar

freshly ground black pepper

1 garlic clove, minced

1/2 small shallot, finely diced

2 cups fresh or frozen strawberries, diced

2–3 teaspoons arrowroot flour mixed in a little cold water

Prepare apples and simmer with lemon juice and sugar in a small saucepan until apples soften. Add balsamic vinegar, pepper, garlic, and shallot. Simmer an additional 5 minutes, add diced strawberries and stir gently. Thicken with a little arrowroot flour mixed in cold water, if necessary. Yields 2 1/2 cups.

CHILLED STRAWBERRY SOUP

The pale pink colour of this soup presents beautifully. I suggest you prepare it early in the day to allow flavours to blend.

2 cups prepared strawberries

1/3 cup sugar

1/2 cup light sour cream

1/2 cup heavy cream, 35% m.f.

1 1/2 cups water

1/2 cup medium sweet red wine

Place rinsed and hulled berries in a blender and purée. Place strawberry purée in a large bowl, whisk in remaining ingredients and chill several hours before serving. Serves 4.

STRAWBERRY RHUBARB SOUP

MURRAY MANOR BED AND BREAKFAST, YARMOUTH, NS

Sweet, yet tart, you may serve this soup warm or chilled. It is very flavourful, easy to prepare, and beautiful in its presentation.

2 cups fresh strawberries, rinsed, hulled, and sliced

1 1/2 cups red rhubarb, in 1–inch slices

1 cup sugar

2 cups water

1 3–inch cinnamon stick

1/2 cup medium sweet red wine

1/2 cup club soda

1/2 cup sour cream

Reserve four strawberries as garnish. Slice remaining strawberries and combine with rhubarb, sugar, water, and cinnamon in a large saucepan. Bring to a boil, reduce heat, and simmer until fruits are tender, approximately 8 minutes. Remove cinnamon stick and purée.

At serving time, stir in wine and club soda. Serve chilled or reheated, garnished with remaining strawberries and a dollop of sour cream. Serves 4.

Prepare Chilled Strawberry Soup early in the day so the flavours will blend ▶

SUMMER SALAD WITH STRAWBERRIES

DARLINGTON'S ON DUKE, HALIFAX, NS

There's no better way to usher in the strawberry season than to prepare this colourful red and green salad. Owner Glenda Allen developed this recipe and uses only freshly picked strawberries.

1/4 cup white vinegar

1/2 cup sugar

1 teaspoon salt

1/2 small red onion, diced

1 teaspoon dry mustard

2 tablespoons water

1 cup vegetable oil

Mesclun or romaine greens to serve 4

1/2 small red onion, sliced in thin rings

1 cup fresh strawberries, rinsed, hulled, and quartered

1/4 cup slivered almonds

croutons

1/4 cup freshly grated Parmesan cheese

In a blender combine vinegar, sugar, salt, red onion, dry mustard, and water and purée. Continue processing, adding oil in a slow stream until emulsified.

Prepare salad greens and toss with remaining red onion rings, strawberries, and almonds. Drizzle with dressing and top with croutons and grated Parmesan. Refrigerate any unused dressing in a tightly capped container. Yields 1 1/4 cups dressing. Serves 4.

◄ *Glenda Allen uses only freshly picked strawberries in her Summer Salad*

STRAWBERRY AND ASSORTED FRUIT TRAY WITH DIP

This is an excellent finger food for a large gathering or buffet, equally popular with children and adults. While any fresh fruit is nice on this tray, I suggest you choose a few with contrasting colours to add to the presentation.

Assorted fresh fruit to serve 6–8 (strawberries, melon chunks, cherries with stems, green grapes, etc.)

1 cup marshmallow ice cream topping

4 ounces cream cheese, at room temperature

Rinse and dry strawberries and cherries, being careful to leave the stems in place. Rinse grapes and separate into small bunches. Cut melon in large slices, remove peel and cube. Arrange fruit in a circle on a large serving tray.

In a medium-sized mixing bowl, beat together the marshmallow topping and cream cheese. Transfer to a small bowl and place in the centre of fruit tray. Yields 1 1/4 cups.
Serves 6–8.

◄ *Strawberries and Assorted Fruit Try with Dip, an excellent finger food for a large gathering*

WILD NEW BRUNSWICK STRAWBERRY SALAD WITH BLUEBERRY DRESSING

ALGONQUIN HOTEL, ST. ANDREWS, NB

Executive chef Willie White calls this his "Parmesan crisp sandwich" and recommends preparing the Local Blueberry Dressing a day in advance so that the flavours will be fully blended.

baby salad greens to serve 4, in bite-sized pieces

1 cup grated Parmesan cheese

freshly ground black pepper

3 ounces cream cheese, softened

12 medium fresh strawberries, rinsed, hulled, and sliced

8 stems fresh chives

edible flowers (chive blossoms or nasturtiums) as garnish

Local Blueberry Dressing, recipe follows

Preheat oven to 400°F. Rinse and dry salad greens, set aside. Spoon grated Parmesan cheese on a Teflon-coated baking sheet in twelve 2 1/2–inch rounds and sprinkle with freshly grated pepper. Bake 4 to 5 minutes until lightly golden brown and firm; remove from oven and cool.

To assemble salads, carefully spread 1/2 teaspoon cream cheese on each Parmesan crisp. Layer each one with strawberries and salad greens, allowing three crisps per serving. Top salads with additional cream cheese and baby greens. Garnish with chives and edible flowers and a drizzle of Local Blueberry Dressing. Serves 4.

Local Blueberry Dressing

1 cup fresh or frozen blueberries

1/4 cup cider vinegar

juice of 1 lemon

1 teaspoon grain-style mustard

3/4 cup canola oil

salt and freshly ground pepper, to taste

Purée blueberries, vinegar, lemon juice, and mustard in a food processor. Continue processing, adding oil in a slow stream until emulsified. Season with salt and pepper, and refrigerate. Yields 1 cup salad dressing.

◀ *Chef Willie White's Wild New Brunswick Strawberry Salad with Blueberry Dressing*

PIES AND BAKED DESSERTS

*O*h, those decadent desserts! In this section, you will find an array of baked goodies, from Mountain Gap Inn's homey Strawberry Rhubarb Pie to the spectacular Strawberries in Phyllo Horns offered up by Michelle LeBlanc of Planters' Barracks Country Inn.

◀ *Liscombe Lodge Fresh Strawberry Pie makes a pleasant addition to any recipe collection*

LISCOMBE LODGE FRESH STRAWBERRY PIE

LISCOMBE LODGE, LISCOMB MILLS, NS

The chef at Liscombe Lodge prides himself on serving Nova Scotian fruits and produce at their peak. I'm sure you will find this strawberry pie a pleasant addition to your recipe collection.

1 quart strawberries, rinsed, hulled, and halved

1 cup sugar

1 cup cold water

3 tablespoons cornstarch

1 teaspoon lemon juice

1 prebaked 9–inch pie shell

whipped cream as garnish (optional)

Crush 1 cup of the strawberries and place in a saucepan. Stir in sugar, water, and cornstarch. Cook over medium heat, stirring occasionally, until thickened and clear, about 25 minutes. Remove from heat, stir in lemon juice, and set aside to cool. Spread remaining berries in pie shell, cover with cooked berries and chill several hours. Serve with a dollop of whipped cream, if desired. Serves 6–8.

GLAZED STRAWBERRY PIE

STEAMERS STOP INN,
GAGETOWN, NB

Innkeeper Pat Stewart serves this pie when berries are abundant, topping it with a decadent dollop of sweetened whipped cream.

pastry for a 9–inch pie

1 quart fresh strawberries

1 cup sugar

3 tablespoons cornstarch

1/4 teaspoon salt

1 teaspoon lemon juice

1 1/2 tablespoon butter

whipping cream (optional)

Prepare pie shell, bake and cool. Clean and hull the berries and cut in half. Cover pastry with a layer of berries, distributing evenly.

Combine sugar, cornstarch, and salt in a medium saucepan. Crush the remaining berries and slowly blend into sugar mixture. Cook over medium heat until thickened and smooth. Reduce heat, cover saucepan and continue to cook for 5 minutes. Remove from heat and stir in lemon juice and butter. Pour over berries in pie shell, being careful to cover them completely. Refrigerate at least 4 hours until set. Serve with sweetened whipped cream, if desired. Serves 6.

STRAWBERRY RHUBARB CRUMBLE

WEST POINT LIGHTHOUSE,
WEST POINT, PEI

Chef Liz Lecky serves this dessert warm from the oven, topped with vanilla ice cream.

1 pint fresh strawberries, rinsed, hulled, and dried

3 cups rhubarb, in 1–inch pieces

3/4 cup sugar

2 tablespoons quick–cooking tapioca

1/2 cup flour

1/4 teaspoon salt

1 teaspoon cinnamon

1/2 cup rolled oats

3/4 cup brown sugar, lightly packed

1/3 cup butter, softened

Preheat oven to 375°F. Lightly butter a shallow baking dish. Prepare fruits and spread in baking dish. Sprinkle with sugar and tapioca. In a medium bowl, mix together flour, salt, cinnamon, rolled oats, brown sugar, and butter using a pastry blender or fingertips. Sprinkle mixture over fruit and pat down lightly. Bake 30–35 minutes. Serve warm or cold. Serves 6.

STRAWBERRY AND WHITE CHOCOLATE NAPOLEONS

CATHERINE McKINNON'S SPOT O' TEA, STANLEY BRIDGE, PEI

Pastry chef Whitney Armstrong prepares wafers made from frozen puff pastry dough for this elegant dessert.

1 package frozen puff pastry dough

Thaw pastry in refrigerator overnight. Preheat oven to 350°F. Roll out pastry thinly on parchment paper, making sure that all the air is removed from the dough by pricking with fork tines. Cut pastry into approximately eighteen 2 1/2–inch rounds, place on an ungreased baking sheet, cover with a second baking sheet and bake 10 minutes. Remove top baking sheet and continue to bake until wafers are light brown in colour, approximately 10 minutes. Remove from oven and cool on a wire rack.

White Chocolate Mousse

1/2 cup heavy cream, 35% m.f.

1/2 cup semi-sweet white chocolate

1 tablespoon powdered gelatin

2 tablespoons hot water

2 cups heavy cream, 35% m.f., whipped

In the top half of a double boiler, blend together the 1/2 cup heavy cream and white chocolate over low heat until chocolate is melted. Be careful not to allow the top half of the double boiler to touch the water or allow the water to boil. Dissolve gelatin in hot water, then stir into cream mixture. Remove from the burner and cool. Fold whipped cream into cooled chocolate mixture and refrigerate.

Strawberry Sauce

1 quart strawberries, rinsed, hulled and quartered

1/2 cup sugar or honey

Combine half of the strawberries and all of the sugar in a saucepan and bring to a boil. Reduce heat and simmer until strawberries are soft, approximately 12 minutes. Remove from heat and strain. Add reserved berries to strawberry sauce and chill.

To serve, pipe or spread a little White Chocolate Mousse around each wafer. Place a wafer on serving plate, top with strawberries, add another wafer and more strawberries. Finish plates by adding a third wafer, a dollop of Mousse and a drizzle of Strawberry Sauce. Serves 4–6.

Strawberry and White Chocolate Napoleons, from Catherine McKinnon's Spot O' Tea ▶
in Stanley Bridge, PEI

STRAWBERRY SHORTCAKE

LOON BAY LODGE, ST. STEPHEN, NB

The chef at Loon Bay Lodge tells us that frozen strawberries can be used for this recipe when fresh berries are unavailable. She usually mashes and freezes a few containers of berries during berry season to have on hand for other times of the year.

1 quart fresh strawberries, washed and hulled or unsweetened frozen strawberries

1/2 cup sugar

2 cups flour

1 1/2 tablespoons baking powder

1/2 teaspoon salt

1/4 cup shortening

1 cup milk

whipped cream as garnish, if desired

Prepare fresh berries or thaw frozen berries in a refrigerator overnight. Add sugar to berries and set aside.

Preheat oven to 400°F. Place flour, baking powder, salt, and shortening in a large bowl. Cut shortening into flour mixture with a pastry blender until well blended. Add milk and stir with a fork until mixture resembles a soft dough. Turn out on a floured board and flatten gently to about 1–inch thickness. Cut with a 3–inch biscuit cutter and bake on an ungreased sheet until light brown, 15–20 minutes. To serve, split biscuits, add strawberries, top with biscuit and garnish with whipped cream. Serves 6–8.

STRAWBERRY RHUBARB PIE

MOUNTAIN GAP INN AND RESORT, SMITHS COVE, NS

Heralding the beginning of summer, the combination of strawberries and rhubarb in this pie offers diners a taste of the best from Mountain Gap's kitchen.

pastry for a double crust 9–inch pie

1 cup sugar

3 tablespoons flour

generous dash nutmeg

3 cups rhubarb, washed and cut in 1–inch pieces

1 cup strawberries, rinsed, hulled, and halved

1 tablespoon butter, melted

Preheat oven to 350°F. Prepare pastry of choice, roll half and fit into a 9–inch pie plate. In a large bowl combine sugar, flour, and nutmeg. Add rhubarb and strawberries, and fill pie shell with fruit mixture. Roll top crust and cover pie, making sure the rim is well sealed. Trim, cut slits in top and brush with butter. Bake 45–60 minutes until fruit is tender and pie is golden brown. Serves 6–8.

Loon Bay Lodge Strawberry Shortcake calls for fresh or frozen berries ▶

MARINATED STRAWBERRIES AND BISCUITS WITH WHIPPED MASCARPONE CHEESE

HOTEL HALIFAX, HALIFAX, NS

At the Hotel Halifax, chef Dale Nichols uses fresh local berries at the peak of their season.

1 quart strawberries, rinsed and hulled

juice of 1 lemon

1/4 cup sugar

Shortcake Biscuits

2 3/4 cups pastry flour

1/4 cup sugar

4 teaspoons baking powder

1 teaspoon salt

10 tablespoons chilled unsalted butter

1 cup heavy cream, 35% m.f. (first amount)

1/4 cup heavy cream, 35% m.f. (second amount)

1/4 cup sugar, for sprinkling

Prepare berries, toss with lemon juice and sugar and set aside.

Preheat oven to 375°F. Thoroughly combine pastry flour, sugar, baking powder, and salt together in a large bowl. Cut in butter with a pastry blender until mealy in texture. Add first amount of cream and stir until dough forms a ball. Roll out 3/4–inch thick on a floured surface and cut in 3–inch rounds. Brush tops with second amount of cream and sprinkle with sugar. Bake on an ungreased cookie sheet

for 5 minutes, reduce heat to 350°F and bake an additional 20–25 minutes until golden.

Whipped Mascarpone Cheese

4 eggs, separated

1/4 cup sugar (first amount)

3/4 cup heavy cream, 35% m.f.

1-pound container mascarpone cheese, at room temperature

1/4 cup sugar (second amount)

Prepare Whipped Mascarpone Cheese by whipping together the egg yolks and first amount of sugar with an electric mixer until pale yellow and fluffy, approximately 10 minutes. Set aside.

In a separate bowl, whip the heavy cream until firm, but not stiff. Fold the cheese into the cream, then fold into the egg yolk mixture. Whip the egg whites until soft peaks form. Sprinkle with second amount of sugar and beat until firm peaks form. Fold into the cheese mixture. Chill several hours.

To assemble desserts, carefully split the shortbread biscuits. Top the bottom half generously with strawberries and a large dollop of mascarpone cheese. Finish the presentation by leaning the biscuit top against the dessert. Serves 6–8.

ORANGE SCENTED STRAWBERRY SHORTCAKES

SEASONS IN THYME, SUMMERSIDE, PEI

*Chef Stefan Czapalay cautions that this is not a rolled biscuit recipe
and the batter will be quite moist.*

2 1/4 cups flour

6 tablespoons sugar

1/4 teaspoon salt

4 1/2 teaspoons baking powder

1 1/2 tablespoons finely grated orange peel

9 tablespoons unsalted butter

1 1/2 cups heavy cream, 35% m.f.

Preheat oven to 350°F. Sift together the flour, sugar, salt, and baking powder. Add orange peel; mix gently. Cut in the butter with a pastry blender until mixture resembles a mealy substance. Add the heavy cream and stir with a wooden spoon until mixture is well blended. With a large spoon, scoop the mixture into eight portions on a cookie sheet and bake for 15 minutes or until golden.

Topping

2 quarts strawberries, rinsed, hulled, and sliced

1 cup sugar (first amount)

1 cup heavy cream, 35% m.f.

2 tablespoons sugar (second amount)

1/2 teaspoon vanilla

Prepare berries and place with first amount of sugar in a large bowl. Allow to stand until the sugar has dissolved and the juices have started to come out of the berries. In a separate bowl whip the cream until almost set, add second amount of sugar and vanilla and continue to beat until cream is stiff. To assemble, place half of a biscuit on the bottom of a plate, top with fresh berries and juices, place the remaining half of biscuit over the top of the berries and place more berries over the top of the biscuit. Garnish with whipped cream. Serves 8.

ORANGE SOUFFLÉ WITH STRAWBERRY SAUCE

KAULBACK HOUSE HISTORIC INN, LUNENBURG, NS

The marriage of orange and strawberry flavours is subtle, yet delightful, in this visually appealing dessert.

3 eggs, separated

3 tablespoons sugar (first amount)

4 teaspoons orange juice (first amount)

1 tablespoon flour

2 tablespoons butter

3 tablespoons orange juice (second amount)

1 tablespoon sugar (second amount)

Prepared Strawberry Sauce (recipe follows)

Preheat oven to 350°F. Separate eggs, and beat whites until frothy, then slowly add sugar and continue to beat until stiff. In a separate bowl whisk together egg yolks, the first amount of orange juice, and flour. Gently fold into egg whites.

Melt butter in a small ovenproof pan. Stir in the second amount of orange juice and 1 tablespoon sugar. Heat in oven until bubbly. Gently slide spoonfuls of egg mixture onto hot butter sauce, allowing approximately 2 tablespoons of egg per soufflé. Bake 15–20 minutes. To serve, divide warm Strawberry Sauce between four serving plates and top with soufflés. Serves 4.

Strawberry Sauce

1 tablespoon butter

1 tablespoon sugar

3 tablespoons orange juice

6 large strawberries, hulled and sliced

In a nonstick pan combine butter, sugar, and orange juice. Cook over medium heat, stirring constantly until slightly thickened. Stir in sliced strawberries and serve warm.

◄ *Orange Soufflé with Strawberry Sauce, a subtle marriage of flavours*

HOTEL BEAUSÉJOUR STRAWBERRY SHORTCAKE

HOTEL BEAUSÉJOUR, MONCTON, NB

For that romantic special occasion pastry chef Tony Holden prepares his shortcakes

2–3 cups fresh strawberry slices

1/4 cup brown sugar

1 teaspoon lemon juice

2 tablespoons freshly squeezed orange juice

Shortcake

4 cups flour

2 tablespoons baking powder

1/4 cup sugar

1/4 teaspoon salt

1 cup butter or margarine

3/4 cup buttermilk

3 eggs, beaten

3/4 cup heavy cream, 35% m.f.

In a large bowl mix together strawberries, brown sugar, lemon and orange juice. Cover and refrigerate to marinate 6 hours.

Preheat oven to 375°F. In a large bowl combine flour, baking powder, sugar, salt, and butter with a pastry blender until mixture resembles crumbs. Combine buttermilk and beaten eggs and add to dry ingredients, mixing to combine. Gently roll out dough on a floured surface to 1 1/2–inch thickness and cut with a 3–inch biscuit cutter. Bake on an ungreased cookie sheet until puffed and browned, approximately 20 minutes. At serving time, slice shortcakes in half, divide berries between halves and over tops. Serve garnished with whipped cream. Serves 8.

WINDS AND BRASS

AMHERST SHORE COUNTRY INN, LORNEVILLE, NS

As pleasing as the resounding strains of a fine symphony, this dessert will fulfil the expectations of the most discriminating sweet lover.

4 ounces light cream cheese, softened

3/4 cup light sour cream

2 tablespoons icing sugar

2 ounces semi-sweet chocolate, melted

1 tablespoon Grand Marnier liqueur

1 1/2 tablespoons Cointreau liqueur

2 cups fresh strawberries, sliced

6 Individual Meringue Shells, recipe follows

grated orange rind and chocolate curls for garnish

Whip the cream cheese until smooth. Stir in sour cream and whip until well blended. Stir in icing sugar, melted chocolate, and liqueurs. Continue to whip until ingredients are well blended and mousse is fluffy. Refrigerate several hours in a well-sealed bowl.

At serving time, gently fold strawberries into mousse. Divide between meringue shells and garnish with grated orange rind and chocolate curls. Serves 6–8.

Individual Meringue Shells

3 egg whites

pinch of cream of tartar

3/4 cup extra-fine or fruit sugar

1/2 teaspoon vanilla

Preheat oven to 250°F. Line a baking sheet with brown paper, and set aside. Beat egg whites and cream of tartar until soft peaks form. Gradually beat in the sugar, continuing to beat until all the sugar has dissolved and the whites are stiff and glossy. Fold in vanilla. For each shell, drop about 1/3 cup meringue onto paper and shape with the back of a spoon into a shell. Bake 1 hour, turn off heat and leave meringues in oven until cooled to room temperature. Yields 8 meringues.

STRAWBERRY TRIFLE

PALLISER RESTAURANT, TRURO, NS

Trifle is an excellent make-ahead dessert. Whether you serve it in individual parfait glasses, as they do at the Palliser, or in a decorative bowl, it is sure to become one of your favourite recipes.

1 prepared sponge cake

1/4 cup sherry

1/2 cup strawberry jam

1 cup heavy cream, 35% m.f., whipped (first amount)

Custard, recipe follows

1 cup fresh or frozen strawberries

1 cup heavy cream, 35% m.f., whipped (second amount)

Slice cake horizontally into two layers. Place bottom layer of cake in a deep serving bowl. Sprinkle with sherry and spread with jam and first amount of whipped cream. Place top layer of cake on top of jam and cream. Prepare custard and spoon over cake; cover with plastic wrap. Chill at least 4 hours or overnight. Serve spooned into individual serving dishes topped with strawberries and second amount of whipped cream, or decorate whole dessert with strawberries and whipped cream, and allow guests to serve themselves. Serves 8–10.

Custard

1/2 cup sugar

3 tablespoons cornstarch

4 egg yolks

3 cups milk

1 teaspoon vanilla

In a heavy-bottomed saucepan, combine sugar and cornstarch. Whisk in egg yolks and milk and cook over medium low heat, stirring constantly until thickened. Remove from heat and stir in vanilla.

The Palliser's Strawberry Trifle is an excellent make-ahead dessert ▶

WILD STRAWBERRY PIE

DUNDEE ARMS, CHARLOTTETOWN, PEI

The chef at Dundee Arms prefers to use wild strawberries in this dish, but he tells us that cultivated berries will also work well.

Pastry

1 1/4 cups flour

pinch of salt

1/2 cup shortening

2–3 tablespoons ice water

Filling

1 1/2 cups sour cream

1/3 cup sugar

1/3 cup orange juice

2 tablespoons cornstarch

1 1/4 cups dry white wine

3/4 cup sugar (2nd amount)

zest of 1 orange

1 quart fresh wild strawberries, rinsed, dried, and hulled

whipped cream for garnish

Preheat oven to 350°F. Combine flour and salt in a mixing bowl. Cut shortening into flour with a pastry blender until mixture is the size of large peas. Do not overmix. Sprinkle with ice water and blend with a fork until absorbed. Form into a ball and roll out on a floured surface. Line a 10–inch pie plate with pastry, prick with a fork, and bake approximately 12 minutes. Remove from oven and cool.

In a saucepan combine sour cream, sugar, orange juice, and cornstarch. Being careful not to allow the mixture to come to a full boil, cook over low heat until thickened. Pour mixture into prepared pie shell.

In a separate saucepan, bring wine, sugar (2nd amount), and orange zest to a boil, reduce heat and cook until mixture is reduced by half, approximately 20 minutes. Remove from heat and stir in strawberries. Set aside 1/2 cup strawberry sauce for garnish, then spoon remaining strawberries over sour cream mixture. Chill pie several hours. To serve, warm reserved sauce, cut pie in 8 wedges, top with a dollop of whipped cream and a spoonful of warm sauce. Serves 8.

Wild Strawberry Pie, a favourite at Dundee Arms in Charlottetown, PEI ▶

STRAWBERRIES IN PHYLLO HORNS

PLANTERS' BARRACKS COUNTRY INN, STARRS POINT, NS

Michelle LeBlanc, innkeeper at "The Barracks" serves this elegant dessert on a bed of Strawberry Coulis decadently drizzled with chocolate. This recipe requires eight to ten metal cream horn moulds which are available in kitchenware specialty stores.

Strawberry Coulis

4 cups fresh strawberries, crushed

1/4 cup sugar

1 teaspoon cornstarch, dissolved in 1 tablespoon cold water

Phyllo Horns

6 sheets phyllo pastry, thawed to room temperature

1/4 cup melted butter

2 tablespoons sugar for sprinkling

1 cup heavy cream, 35% m.f., whipped

fresh strawberries, as garnish

2 ounces semi-sweet chocolate, melted

Prepare Strawberry Coulis early in the day. In a medium saucepan heat strawberries over medium heat and cook until berries have softened. Strain berries, discarding seeds. Place the strawberry juice over low heat, stir in sugar and cornstarch mixture, and cook until liquid is thick and bubbly. Remove from burner and cool.

Preheat oven to 350°F. Take the first sheet of phyllo pastry, place it on a work surface and using a pastry brush, lightly coat with butter and sprinkle with sugar. Immediately top with another layer of pastry and repeat this process. Do not butter or sprinkle sugar on the top or sixth layer. Cut pastry to cover 8–10 cream horn moulds. Grease each mould with a little butter and wrap with pastry, tucking loose ends in place on underside. Place on a greased cookie sheet and bake until golden brown, approximately 10 minutes. Remove from oven and allow to cool before carefully removing moulds.

To serve, pipe each cone full of whipped cream and garnish with fresh strawberries and Strawberry Coulis. Drizzle with melted chocolate. Serve immediately. Serves 8–10.

◄ *Strawberries in Phyllo Horns, an elegant dish served on a bed of Strawberry Coulis and drizzled with chocolate*

STRAWBERRY CRÈME BRÛLÉE

KAULBACK HOUSE HISTORIC INN, LUNENBURG, NS

Innkeeper Karen Padovani cautions that you must watch carefully so as not to burn the sugar. In testing I found that a Corningware-style dish worked well.

1/2 cup light sour cream

2 tablespoons brown sugar

2 cups sliced strawberries

4 whole strawberries, for garnish

Preheat broiler. Spread the sour cream in a broiler-safe glass pan. Sprinkle with brown sugar and broil only until sugar has caramelized, approximately 1 1/2 minutes. Cool slightly, then add strawberries, tossing to coat. Refrigerate 8 hours and serve, garnished with a whole strawberry. Yields 4 servings.

FRESH STRAWBERRY PIE

LOON BAY LODGE, ST. STEPHEN, NB

Geraldine Alexander of Loon Bay Lodge serves her guests this sumptuous pie when berries are at their peak.

2 quarts fresh strawberries

1 cup sugar

2 tablespoons cornstarch dissolved in 3 tablespoons cold water

1 prebaked 9–inch pie shell

whipped cream for garnish (optional)

Prepare berries by hulling, rinsing, and drying slightly. In a large bowl, mash half of the berries and place in a large saucepan. Over medium heat, bring berries to a boil, reduce heat and simmer 10 minutes. Remove berries from the stove and strain. Return syrup to saucepan, add sugar and bring back to a boil. Stir in cornstarch mixture and continue to cook until sauce is thickened. Remove from burner, place in a bowl and cool.

Reserve a few berries for garnish. Slice remaining berries and add to cooled syrup. Pour into a cold prebaked pie shell and garnish with whipped cream and a few berries. Serves 6–8.

Be careful not to burn the sugar when preparing this Strawberry Crème Brûlée ▶

CHILLED DESSERTS

*L*ooking for the perfect ending to a summer dinner? What better way to finish your meal than by enjoying a cool dessert? From the Strawberry Mousse at the Carriage House Inn in Fredericton to the delectable Strawberry Cheesecake from Summerside's Seasons in Thyme, I'm sure you'll find this section crammed with choices for the perfect dessert.

◄ The recipe for Fresh Fruit Grande calls for chocolate shells available in supermarkets or specialty shops

FRESH FRUIT GRANDE

PANSY PATCH, ST. ANDREWS, NB

The chef at the Pansy Patch tells us that chocolate shells are available in large supermarkets or in specialty food stores.

Strawberry Coulis

2 cups fresh strawberries, rinsed, hulled, and quartered

3/4 cup water (first amount)

1/4 cup sugar, or to taste

2–3 tablespoons cornstarch

3 tablespoons cold water (second amount)

1 1/2 cups fresh strawberries, rinsed, hulled, and quartered

6 bitter-sweet chocolate shells

1/2 cup heavy cream, 35% m.f., whipped

chocolate curls, for garnish

Prepare Strawberry Coulis by placing 2 cups of berries in a saucepan with the first amount of water and sugar. Bring to a boil, reduce heat and simmer until strawberries are softened, approximately 3 minutes. Combine cornstarch with the second amount of water, add to saucepan and cook until slightly thickened. Remove from burner, cool slightly and purée. Chill sauce.

At serving time, divide 1 1/2 cups fresh berries between chocolate shells. Drizzle a small amount of Strawberry Coulis on individual serving plates, top with filled chocolate shells, and decorate with whipped cream and chocolate curls. Serves 6.

HARBOURVIEW CRÈME FRAÎCHE AND FRESH STRAWBERRIES

HARBOURVIEW INN, SMITHS COVE, NS

Mona Webb at the Harbourview Inn felt this scrumptious dessert was "too simple." Well, I like "simple," and I'm sure you will too!

1 quart fresh strawberries

1/2 cup crème fraîche* or sour cream

3–4 tablespoons brown sugar

Rinse and dry strawberries, leaving the hulls intact. Place in a shallow bowl suitable for table presentation. Place crème fraîche in a small bowl and the brown sugar in a separate small bowl. To serve, allow guests to dip strawberries, first in crème fraîche and then in brown sugar. Serves 4.

* Crème fraîche is a mature, thickened cream that is easy to prepare and will keep refrigerated for up to one week. Simply place 1 cup heavy cream (35% m.f.) in a glass bowl, stir in 2 tablespoons buttermilk and cover. Allow to stand at room temperature, approximately 70°F, from 8–24 hours. Stir well, cover and refrigerate.

CARRIAGE HOUSE INN STRAWBERRY MOUSSE

CARRIAGE HOUSE INN, FREDERICTON, NB

Innkeeper Joan Gorham likes this dessert because it calls for fresh or frozen berries. If you are using frozen berries, be sure that they have not been presweetened.

2 1/2 cups fresh or frozen strawberries

3 tablespoons unflavoured gelatin

1/4 cup cold water (first amount)

1 cup water (second amount)

1 cup sugar

1 teaspoon rum

1 cup heavy cream, 35% m.f.

additional whipped cream and fresh berries (optional)

Purée prepared berries in a blender and set aside. In a separate bowl, sprinkle gelatin over the first amount of cold water to soften; let stand 5 minutes. In a saucepan bring the second amount of water to a boil; remove from heat and stir in sugar and softened gelatin, stirring until gelatin and sugar have dissolved. Cool mixture.

Combine cooled gelatin and puréed strawberries, and stir in rum. Place bowl in a pan of ice water to speed setting. Beat cream into soft peaks. Fold whipped cream into strawberry mixture until no streaks of white remain. Pour into a decorative serving bowl or individual dishes and chill until set, approximately 4 hours. Garnish with additional whipped cream and fresh strawberries, if desired. Serves 6–8.

STRAWBERRY CHEESECAKE

SEASONS IN THYME, SUMMERSIDE, PEI

This is an unbaked cheesecake, easy to prepare and beautiful in its presentation. For the photograph, chef Stefan Czapalay topped the dessert with a Chocolate Ganache and served it on a bed of chocolate sauce.

Crust

2 cups Oreo cookie crumbs

1/2 cup butter, melted

Strawberry Coulis

5 teaspoons powdered gelatin

3–4 tablespoons cold water

3 cups fresh strawberries, sliced

1/2 cup sugar

Cheesecake

20 ounces cream cheese, at room temperature

1/2 cup sugar

2 drops of vanilla

2 1/2 cups prepared Strawberry Coulis

In a small bowl combine Oreo cookie crumbs and melted butter. Press into the bottom of an 9-inch springform pan. Refrigerate until set.

Sprinkle gelatin over cold water and set aside to soften. Place strawberries in a saucepan, sprinkle with sugar and simmer over low heat until the juice starts to come out of the berries. Turn the heat to medium high, and cook stirring constantly, for 4 minutes. Stir in softened gelatin mixture and continue to cook, approximately 1 minute longer until gelatin is completely dissolved. Remove pot from burner and strain sauce through a sieve. Cool.

In a separate bowl beat the cream cheese with sugar and vanilla until light and fluffy. Add 1 1/3 cups of Strawberry Coulis to cheese mixture, beating until fully blended. Pour onto prepared cheesecake crust and refrigerate until partially set, approximately 3 hours. Garnish by glazing top of cheesecake with remaining Strawberry Coulis, and refrigerate until set. Serves 8.

Seasons in Thyme's Strawberry Cheesecake is easy to prepare and beautiful to present ▶

ENGLISH SUMMER PUDDING

SALMON RIVER HOUSE COUNTRY INN, SALMON RIVER, NS

Celebrate the first berries of the season by preparing this traditional English dessert. The innkeeper notes that fresh raspberries will produce equally satisfying results.

2 quarts fresh strawberries, rinsed and hulled

1/2 cup sugar

8 slices stale white bread, crusts removed

1/2 cup milk

1 1/4 cups heavy cream, 35% m.f.

2 tablespoons sugar (optional)

Prepare strawberries and place in a large bowl. Sprinkle with sugar and stir gently to dissolve sugar completely. Butter, then line a deep, round bowl with plastic wrap. Moisten bread slices with milk and line the bowl snugly, reserving two slices for the top of the pudding.

Pour strawberries into the lined dish and cover with reserved bread slices. Cover with plastic wrap. Refrigerate at least 8 hours or overnight.

Whip cream and sweeten to taste. At serving time, uncover pudding and gently turn out onto a serving plate; remove plastic wrap. Serve in individual dessert cups, garnished with a dollop of whipped cream. Serves 6–8.

STRAWBERRY CHANTILLY

FALCOURT INN, NICTAUX, NS

This is a versatile dessert. Chef Brian Veinott suggests that you serve it on a slice of angel food cake, meringue, or in prepared sponge dessert cups.

6–8 servings angel food cake

2 cups heavy cream, 35% m.f.

1 scant cup icing sugar

1/2 cup fresh strawberries, mashed

6 whole strawberries with caps for garnish

Divide angel food cake between 6 serving plates. Whip cream until soft peaks form. Slowly sprinkle in sugar while continuing to whip until stiff. Gently fold mashed berries into cream mixture.

Put mixture into a piping bag and decorate cake pieces, or spoon a small amount of cream mixture onto cake pieces. Garnish each plate with a fanned fresh strawberry. Serves 6–8.

◄ *Chef Brian Veinott's Strawberry Chantilly*

STRAWBERRY FLAMBÉ

PANSY PATCH, ST. ANDREWS, NB

This dessert makes a very spectacular table-side presentation. The chef at the Pansy Patch serves his desserts garnished with whipped cream and a whole strawberry.

6 tablespoons water

3 tablespoons sugar

6 large strawberries, rinsed, hulled, and halved

1 1/2 ounces brandy

scoop of vanilla ice cream

Prepare the syrup by heating the water and sugar in a skillet until the mixture almost crystallizes. Add strawberries and heat on high for 3 minutes. Remove pan from burner, add brandy and ignite. Serve flaming strawberry sauce over a dish of vanilla ice cream. Serves 1.

▲ *Strawberry Flambé makes a spectacular table-side presentation*

STRAWBERRIES IN SHERRY CREAM

MURRAY MANOR BED AND BREAKFAST, YARMOUTH, NS

Joan Semple of the Murray Manor serves this dessert mid-way through the berry season when the berries are their sweetest. She cautions that when making the custard, you should not allow the water to boil at more than a simmer and the bottom of the insert pan should not touch the water.

4 egg yolks

1 cup sugar

3/4 cup dry sherry

2 tablespoons brandy

6 cups fresh strawberries

1 cup heavy cream, 35% m.f., whipped

Beat egg yolks until thick and pale yellow in colour, approximately 8 minutes. Add sugar and continue beating until smooth. Stir in sherry and brandy. Place egg mixture in the top of a double boiler and cook over hot, but not boiling water, stirring constantly until thick. Transfer to a bowl to cool.

Wash, hull, and dry strawberries. Place 8 berries aside to use as a garnish, then halve the remaining berries. Whip the cream until very stiff and fold into the cooled custard. Gently stir in strawberry halves and chill.

Divide between individual dessert dishes and decorate with whole berries. Serves 8.

Strawberries in Sherry Cream, an ideal dessert when berries are at their sweetest ▶

KIWIS AND STRAWBERRIES IN CHAMPAGNE

LISCOMBE LODGE,
LISCOMB MILLS, NS

Elegance and simplicity — this dessert presents beautifully in a stemmed glass! The chef at Liscombe Lodge serves it when strawberries are bountiful.

2 kiwi, peeled and cut in 1/4 inch slices

1/4 cup sugar

2 cups fresh strawberries, cut in half

3/4 cup champagne

Place prepared kiwi in a large bowl and sprinkle with sugar. Let stand 30 minutes. Combine strawberries and kiwi then divide between six dessert dishes. At serving time, drizzle champagne over fruit. Serves 6.

FRESH STRAWBERRY FOOL

ACTON'S GRILL AND CAFÉ,
WOLFVILLE, NS

At Acton's, the ever popular "Fool" is served using fresh fruit of the season.

5 cups hulled strawberries

1 cup sugar

1 teaspoon rum or brandy, optional

1 cup heavy cream, 35% m.f.

fresh mint for garnish

Set aside a few whole berries for garnish. In a food processor or blender, purée remaining berries. Stir in sugar and liquor and set aside at room temperature for 1 hour, stirring occasionally. Cover and refrigerate several hours.

Just before serving, whip cream and gently fold into strawberry purée. Turn into individual serving bowls, garnish with whole berries and mint. Serves 6.

Kiwis and Strawberries in Champagne combines elegance with simplicity ▶

DARLINGTON'S ON DUKE MARINATED STRAWBERRIES

DARLINGTON'S ON DUKE, HALIFAX, NS

At Darlington's on Duke they serve this elegant dessert with either dark or white chocolate mousse. Either version is delectable.

1 quart fresh strawberries, rinsed and hulled

2 tablespoons sugar

1/4 cup balsamic vinegar

Dark Chocolate Mousse (recipe follows)

chocolate shavings and mint leaves, as garnish

Quarter berries, sprinkle with sugar and drizzle with vinegar. Toss lightly to coat and refrigerate 2 hours.

Divide berries between stemmed glasses. Top with chocolate mousse and garnish with chocolate shavings and mint leaves.
Serves 6–8.

Dark Chocolate Mousse *(supplied by author)*

1 cup heavy cream, 35% m.f.

1/4 cup super-fine sugar

2 egg yolks

2 ounces dark semi-sweet chocolate

Whip cream in a chilled bowl until thickened, then gradually add in sugar, beating until stiff. Refrigerate until needed. Place yolks in a small mixing bowl and beat on medium speed until lemon coloured, approximately 3 minutes. Melt chocolate to a smooth consistency in a double boiler. Cool slightly, then stir into egg mixture. Fold whipped cream into chocolate, a few spoonfuls at a time, until completely blended. Refrigerate 2 hours before serving. Yields 1 1/4 cups.

The Marinated Strawberries at Darlington's on Duke can be served with either white or ▶ dark chocolate

WHITE CHOCOLATE TOWERS WITH STRAWBERRY BAVAROIS

SEASONS IN THYME, SUMMERSIDE, PEI

Chef Stefan Czapalay makes Chocolate Towers by painting layers of tempered chocolate over plastic cylinders. Less adventuresome cooks can spoon the Strawberry Bavarois into prepared chocolate shells.

Chocolate Towers

8 ounces white chocolate (first amount)

4 ounces white chocolate (second amount)

8 strips of plastic, 3 x 6 inches, formed into cylinders

To temper chocolate: In a double boiler, bring 3 cups of water to a boil, then place the first amount of chocolate in a perfectly dry bowl or insert, and set directly upon the boiling water. Turn off the heat and stir until the chocolate is completely melted. Add the second amount of chocolate and stir until melted and the temperature of the combined chocolates has reached 89°F.

Using a small spatula or knife, spread several thin coats of chocolate onto each plastic cylinder. Reserve in a cool, dry area but do not refrigerate.

Strawberry Bavarois

1 1/2 cups fresh strawberries, rinsed, hulled and sliced

5 tablespoons sugar

1 envelope powdered gelatin

2 cups heavy cream, 35% m.f.

fresh strawberries, for garnish

Place strawberries in a medium-sized saucepan, sprinkle with sugar and simmer over low heat until the juice starts to come out of the berries. Turn the heat to medium high and cook, stirring constantly, for 4 minutes. Remove pot from burner and strain sauce through a sieve. This should yield 1 cup strawberry sauce. Divide sauce, keeping 1/2 cup hot and chilling the other half. Soften the gelatin in the chilled sauce, allowing it to stand 5 minutes. Fold gelatin mixture into hot sauce and stir until gelatin is fully dissolved. Cool mixture.

Whip cream until stiff, then gently fold in cooled strawberry sauce.

To serve, carefully remove plastic from hardened chocolate towers and fill with Strawberry Bavarois. Garnish with fresh strawberries. Serves 8.

◄ *Painted layers of tempered chocolate enhance chef Stefan Czapalay's White Chocolate Towers with Strawberry Bavarois*

FALCOURT STRAWBERRY DESSERT

FALCOURT INN, NICTAUX, NS

Chef Brian Veinott serves this eye-catching dessert in elegant stemmed glasses. If the strawberry variety you use is sweet, you might want to decrease the amount of sugar in the recipe.

1 quart fresh strawberries, rinsed, hulled, and halved

1/3 cup kirsch liqueur

1/3 cup sugar

1 cup coffee cream, 18% m.f.

fresh mint leaves, as garnish

Combine strawberries, kirsch and sugar; place in a large glass bowl and refrigerate 1–2 hours.

After strawberries have marinated, spoon into champagne glasses, drizzle with cream, and garnish with fresh mint. Serves 6–8.

Falcourt Strawberry Dessert, an eye-catching dish served in an elegant stemmed glass ▶

INDEX